The Watchful Heart Recedes

poems by

Ellen Gerneaux Woods

Finishing Line Press
Georgetown, Kentucky

The Watchful Heart
Recedes

Copyright © 2021 by Ellen Gerneaux Woods
ISBN 978-1-64662-713-4 First Edition
All rights reserved under International and Pan-American Copyright Conventions. No part of this book may be reproduced in any manner whatsoever without written permission from the publisher, except in the case of brief quotations embodied in critical articles and reviews.

ACKNOWLEDGMENTS

I thank the following journals for their publication of individual poems:

"Monterey Aquarium", *In Laymen's Terms*, May 2018
"Distracted", *Pudding Magazine* #68, December 2019
"Agency", *Is It Hot in Here?* Anthology, January 2020

I am grateful also to family and friends, the Master Poetry group, my writing and spiritual teachers, and especially my daughter Liliana.

Publisher: Leah Huete de Maines
Editor: Christen Kincaid
Cover Art: Michele Benzamin-Miki
Author Photo: Natasha Shocron
Cover Design: Elizabeth Maines McCleavy

Order online: www.finishinglinepress.com
also available on amazon.com

Author inquiries and mail orders:
Finishing Line Press
PO Box 1626
Georgetown, Kentucky 40324
USA

Table of Contents

Monterey Aquarium 1

September Walnut Drop 3

Competitive Leanings 4

Wild Iris Fears 5

What the Crows See 6

A Mother's Lament 7

Trophy to a Mother's Rage 8

Modern Choices 9

Culling the Files 11

Through It Together 13

Criminal Justice 101 15

Agency 16

Pandemic Lunch Hour 17

Family Campout: Summer 1950 18

Ode to the Dinner Bell 19

Distracted 20

*For my grandmother Bobo, Bertha Gerneaux Davis (1893-1952)
who inspired me with her published books of poetry
and her love for her family.*

Monterey Aquarium
 —*for my daughter*

    i

once we were of the sea
birthed in water

our gills found our breath
amphibian
  reptile
    mammal

    ii

custody schedule
every other long weekend

we drive south
101 to 156
Monterey

enter massive
doors to the dark
walls of lighted tanks

swarms of jellyfish
contract
  pulsate
    wave their tentacles

umbrella bell bodies
moon jellies never
leave their tribe

millions of years
luminescent
emitting the light

iii

jellies 98% water
humans 72%
what have we lost?

September Walnut Drop

walnuts lie among leaves
hard round trip-hazards so many
that picking up several
doesn't make a dent

my daughter kicks a soccer ball
doesn't fall or even notice
black annoyances
in her path

the landlord offers a nickel
for each one collected
Lil's ten-year-old self
recognizes a deal
fills the metal pail

in no time she has one-hundred walnuts
five-dollars' worth immediately exchanged
for three pepperoni slices
at Berkeley Bowl

single mother wanting more
I sneak a few into my pocket
sprain my ankle on another
my thoughts on walnut pie

Competitive Leanings
—For Lil

in the middle of a conversation
laying out a twelve-year-old's explanation
of pitching strategy
players' parents rapt

you
glowing in your white uniform
and well-worn cleats
raise up your arm
  mitt in hand
    catch the ball that comes your way
sent by a sidelined teammate
no *think fast* warning offered

you hardly blink
  or even notice your natural gift
    until admirers' applause erupts
and you blush

your comrade scowls

Wild Iris Fears

it spreads wide
over the sidewalk
base of thin leaves
shooting upward
almost to my heart

dozens of blooms
narrow petals in gold
alabaster angular face
  lifting
   needing no tending
year after year

I pick a bouquet
  within the hour it droops
   lifeless
the iris wilts

sever their connections
  with the mother plant
  they lose conviction

leave them in the ground
  they thrive
  for generations

What the Crows See

on her upstairs deck she sits on
the plastic Adirondack chair
its armrests permanently marked

with cigarette stains left
by daughter's nasty ways   scrubbed clean now
embedded even

in her absence   beloved girl
on her own   gone now
halfway across the country

she closes her eyes   allows
a smile to rest on her lips   enjoying
her solitude while she looks up

at the ancient redwood where we gather
content to wait until
a penny or a silver ribbon pulls us

to claim it   releases us from our perch
to deliver the gift
to her chair   we watch

visit her in twos
sometimes in a flock
we meet her eyes telling her

the message we bring
a new beginning   a birth   she
thanks us with a nod

A Mother's Lament

asleep in my bed
comforted by down
and darkness
I hear your cry

a screech like sudden
train brakes
I rise up   your bed is empty
you no longer live here

I go to the deck
squint at the yard
scan for intruders
no one is there

 instinct propels me
anybody need help?
a bulky mass of fur slinks down
the trunk of the ancient redwood

a cat or a raccoon
unwelcome in the tree
fought off by a raucous
den of squirrels

the smell of danger
triggers impulse
to protect the young
they shriek for survival

I look on useless
no one to protect
but me
the watchful heart recedes

lungs expand   fill with
shiver of night air
neighbor's roof edged
with amber dawn

Trophy to a Mother's Rage

Did you see them coming I asked her,
days after it was over
stroking her twenty-something hair

I saw them Mommy
but I didn't want to be a racial profiler.
They looked like they were in grade school
so I ignored them.

Baby our long time neighbor said *watch your back.*
No one deserves what you got
Cross the street if anyone comes towards you.
Yell for help. Give them your money, your phone.
They were wrong, but you're alive.

He sucked his teeth
uttered a closed-mouth grunt barely audible
looked down shaking his head.

in a dream that night I saw them
and many nights after

street lights pierced their ghostly bodies
strung upside down
by the laces of their Nike kicks
tagging the spot of their violence.

all the stolen loot phones cash
fell fast from their pockets
while they screamed for their mama
who stood below
shoulder to shoulder with me

Modern Choices

Ralphie arrived by rental car
Lil and husband Bri driving eighteen-
hundred miles from Kansas
Lil's birthplace
before the California adoption

fate took her back to try Midwestern life
now she was coming home

Lil knew Ralphie was her baby
his tail thumped   they locked eyes in the aisles
of the Kansas Animal Shelter

pudgy American Bulldog
a placid friendly breed
Ralphie quivered as he left the sunflower state
coaxed into car with cardboard boxes
stuffed garbage bags   a suitcase

along the way folks balked when they saw him
thinking him an oversize Pit Bull yet
when he exited the car days later in Berkeley
kids shouted Gordo and embraced him
like a favorite uncle

Lil stayed when Bri went back to Kansas
Ralphie thrived in South Berkeley   object
of her devotion

in time she found a new man
they fell in love
his landlord said *No Dogs Allowed*
she had to choose

Ralphie departed in his new owner's car
quivering as he stared with onyx pools
Lil and I stood fixed in the drive
wet-faced and aching   arms raised in goodbye

I found him a good home, Mom   she was firm
just like you found me a good home
good comes from good: we know that.

Culling the Files

Now that I'm ready
I lift the gold scarf from
my black file cabinet
and look in the top drawer

the information
untended
since my last thinning

no longer cramping my view
marriage   divorce
shredded years ago

details of my single-mom life
pushed to the back:
landlord's nasty letters
the Rent Board's abiding protection

letters from my beloved daughter:
U.S. Army, Honorable Discharge
at nineteen; home at twenty-two
military husband in tow   no benefits

pamphlets on birth control
surgeries she survived
her eyes screamed loss
files on pets
adopted to soothe the ache

college apps to try again
GI Bill denied
ledger on son-in-law's loans
not repaid before he walked out

I hand-tear memories for recycling
the mass diminished
by soaking, wrung out
carried to outside bins.

we three built courage
in eight-hundred-square-feet
he to leave, she to stay, me to forgive.

Through It Together

Thanks for this morning. We got through it together
my twenty-seven-year-old daughter texted

divorce papers filed today   he left three years ago
she now in love with a better man

I once inquired *when?*   she reared up
like a horse startled by a moving car
whites of her eyes revealing it was too much
too big   I needed to back off

until today   she called to ask me to
drive her to the courthouse to record
the divorce papers prepared *in pro per*

she climbed in   mute   caffeine driven
fingernails bitten back

the clerk stamped papers   gave us copies
Lil's jaw was tight   she paced the hallway

at Alameda County Sheriff's office
stood in line too long   told
No, gotta mail to Kansas, Riley County

the wait too much   our shouts erupted
my voice shrill   hers staccato

until Crystal, blessed Crystal
Riley County Sheriff's Clerk
returned my call
gave specific mailing instructions
We'll take care of it hon

Mom, Lil said, *I'm exhausted,*
I feel your anxiety   you feel mine
I can't stand it.   I need to go home.
Now.

Alone I felt the regret
old patterns arose from my own losses

until I got her text.

Criminal Justice 101

she calls
I hold my breath
newly enlivened my daughter thrilled
to be back in school
A+ student

Mom I'm in court in Martinez
interviewed expert on gang-related homicide
witness claims
he was jumped   his buddy murdered
he looks scared   hiding in his hoodie

I share her excitement
listen for her discomfort

two thugs
orange prison suits   chains and all
.
involved   assertive   compassionate
so unlike the Lil assaulted
by two teenagers those years ago
three blocks from home

that Lil wouldn't talk
left me mute as well
her refusal to be touched   my arms aching

Gotta go mom,
tomorrow we go to the morgue
I can't wait

I breathe in gratitude

Agency

You are approaching the age
 it began
where should you need it
it cautiously proceeded
your wishes should be
known by your doctor

the email from Kaiser
gives me fifteen options
of days/times to attend
Life Care Planning

I am admonished to
bring along my agent

thoughts of the goldenrod
Advance Care Directive Kit
on my To-Do list for years

Cremation Plan paid in full
Will prepared   signed
to protect six-year-old Lil
now twenty-seven/married

I have no agent
older siblings far away
friends yes agents no

Lil is who I need to choose
and yet unthinkable
child as parent

when I was six
my father's fear prepared
me for mother's death
as long as I can remember

In her seventies she died peacefully.

Pandemic Lunch Hour

five months in I take the risk
drive to Walnut Creek
her husband greets with air hugs
she appears   bear hugs

three dining room chairs hauled out
under the weeping willow   masked
blue tarp in grass   six foot circle
Bakesale Betty's bag in the middle

Lil pulls out three white bags
masks are lowered

I recite our family grace
Anthony smiles indulgently   not into prayers
Lil doesn't say the words she knows by heart

Anthony peers into his bag   *awesome*
Lil licks her lips   winks at me

fried chicken sandwiches
balanced on knees
we toast the future   chow down

talk Trump   shake with laughter
remember how it was
wonder how it will be

Anthony cleans up like the decent man he is
I drive back to Berkeley chanting
Prayer of Loving Kindness

May all beings be peaceful
May all beings be happy
May all beings awaken to the light of their true nature
May all beings be free

Campout
    Summer 1950, Brown County Park
    —*for Daddy, Mother, Woody and Cari*

four-fifths of family
number five behind camera
captured with love

mother at ease   dark hair
before sickness took over

three absorbed:
newspaper—mom/older sis
comics—big brother
me—engaged with earth

immersed
collecting leaves   stones   bugs
brown glass bottle
holding earth's bounty

Daddy documents
makes memories
did he know what was next?

Ode to the Dinner Bell
 —*for Mother (1915-1990)*

your considerable fingers
freshly manicured
clutch the wooden handle
your wrist flips back and forth
intensely calls us home

brass cradle
hollow cup
vibrates
uvula claps
resonant call
at 6 o'clock

I crouch
in my hiding tree
want to stay
want to go
hoping for sustenance

I am flooded
with smells
baked potatoes
meatloaf
cherry pie

brass cradle
hollow cup
vibrates
uvula claps
at 6:03

Distracted

On my deck this morning
I air out the mildew cover,
shake the pages of my mother's cookbook.

I am saddened by my dearth of memories
of this woman who loved me
in her way.

Distracted, I see, too late, the green and white flutter
taking to the air like butterflies, while I am helpless
to their lighting in the yard.

S & H Green Stamps saved deliberately
in the back of the cookbook
acquired from the weekly shop

at Livingston's Market on Third Street
exchanged for plates with the red apple pattern
two green leaves and green line edging.

Plates that served up suppers for her family
where Daddy talked about his day at work.
Dinners where I felt her anger and pride

in the muscle of her mind, held back,
wanting expression, subsumed by her allegiance
to her duty as a mother and a housewife

I search for the fallen stamps
Some have melted into damp grass
Others are intact.

Ellen Gerneaux Woods writes poetry and memoir. Her book, *Warriors in Transition: A Memoir in Twenty-Eight Stories* was published in 2014 and her work appears in print and online publications including *Inquiring Mind, Blood and Thunder: Musings on the Art of Medicine, About Place Journal, Marin Poetry Center 2018 Anthology, The Bezine, Pudding Magazine, Is it Hot in Here Anthology, Persimmon Tree,* and *Poems of Political Protest Anthology*, among others.

She has received prizes from the Soul-Making Literary Competition (2011-2014) and Mendocino Coast Writer's Conference.

Ellen serves as a judge of the Prose Poem category for the Soul-Making Literary Competition and Co-chair of the Soul-Making 2020 Zoom Awards event. She has curated written work for Bay Area Generations. She organizes and attends local writing retreats and encourages writers across genres and levels of experience to participate.

She is a retired county psychiatric social worker, mother of one adult daughter, and a practitioner of meditation. She lives in Oakland, CA.

www.ingramcontent.com/pod-product-compliance
Lightning Source LLC
LaVergne TN
LVHW041524070426
835507LV00013B/1813